"Memoirs of a Barista"

By

Sue-Lynn Ansari

Memoirs of a Barista

Dedicated to my Grandma Ruth for teaching me how to make coffee, how to sew, and how to talk to anyone. I miss you and your letters in our mailbox every week. Your quilts kept us warm, your from scratch pies kept our bellies full, and your love is worn on all your children, grandchildren, and great grandchildren.

Table of Contents

Preface

Firstly, I must say I have a deep respect
for coffee and the notions surrounding it.
I love the smell the taste the feel and the
color of it. I was an artist thrown in the
mix with coffee which brought us closer
together in our respects and relationship.
I've served many walks of people and have
gotten to share with them my personal craft-
ing with this amazing thing called coffee.
This story was
created and based on real people and
specifically tells a story from the
perspective of a Barista. Barista is
an Italian term which means to serve or keep bar.
This Barista is not based on no one single person,
but rather a compilation of Barista's I had witnessed in
their work, life, and cafe presence. From the
antics going on to get everyone through their
day, customers and us alike, to the side bar
conversations there was always music to sway.
Their lives have touched me so, and has caused
me to ink-bleed this tale to share a perspective,
a view because who knows maybe in 50 years the
thought of coffee may be just be a thought between
me and you.

Chapter 1 : Day 1

"AH!" Just jumped up out of bed 2:00 O'CLOCK Ow my head...Damn how to get back to sleep again how can I win.....Thoughts of home, thoughts of school, memories of the guy I served.. a tool.......Black tea.....black tea......back tea.....Zzzzzzzzzzzzz. Oh my God Now it hits the fan It's 4:22 and I'm late again. Shower splash, dash of perfume try to hide the wreaking fumes of laundry two weeks old coffee grinds, mocha, ohhh I found a dollar feel just fine. Breakfast thoughts tempt me so don't want to look like I do blow. Why did I ever choose this job has me set on Go-Go-Go. Hope the car starts hope it's still parked there how's my make-up fix the hair. Stuff it in my hat flow with the health code City of angels work with what they wrote. 4:42 On my way two exits left on this curse-ed freeway. Should I call say I'm late why do I seem to ask this everyday? Will I change is there hope, or have I reached the end of my rope stop this now almost there screw the call listen to what's on the air. DJ soothes with morning jams knows how I hit the wall in slams. Give me a smile let me wear it through least for 4 hours when I'm out & through. 5:02 just pulled in why do I feel like I've committed sin. Mirror glance, apron check, grab the face off of my tape deck. Pioneer says it all as I make my way please don't fall. "Ralph I'm so sorry I didn't call....I know I'm late but consider the state I was dialing your name dropped my phone would have been fine but I wasn't alone on the road I mean on the freeway went a black and white rolled on me oh so tight i prayed on spot I wouldn't see a flash of his light....but I'm here, ready to go what do you need before I flow?" 5:09 a.m. man walks in causes us both to smile like sin "Let's make our day" as Ralph whispers my way. My eyes roll and I step into the cage swallow the conversation that was building rage. Caramel macchiato course it would be, and now he wants to coach like he knows me. "Sweetie" he says, like I'm his coffee whore "I'd appreciate some extra sauce if you can put in more" Smile like I didn't notice cause comments there will be more just like him just as bad, simmer down don't get mad. "Here you go" with a smile "Sorry you had to wait a while." Man I'm good like a rock always able to walk and talk. 7:00 am in the trenches room of tools and java wenches keep head down eyes even low as I pour, stir, and make espresso flow. Oh my word here it comes heels click clack here she comes miss sugar-free vanilla with 2 shots, oh and non-fat milk still has wants a-lot. Click-clack click-clack as she makes her attack "Would you mind to put these two sugar-lows in my bev" I smile as the pulse begins to rev. I rip the packet and swallow hard for I know this type she'll throw a wild card. "Can you make it extra hot like to a degree of 220 make sure it's no less for it's my venti" The dragon scales begin to show through the airbrush matted glow as she stares me down through my work and her drink slips back down the lane behind two jerks. I mean a short hazelnut latte and a skinny cappuccino for a not so skinny Joe-blow. "Here you go miss, sorry for the wait" as I pray inside she doesn't get irate. Whew zombie number 67 makes his way over to save the day. She sips the drink and walks away with Mr. Z unaware of in her nose the snow I see. One-in-a-million angel city. All struggling to be beauty, talent, and witty I'm so friggin sick of this city. Self absorbed will they grow not by my words this isn't my show can't save them all they choose to fall away from society what do they think of me the one here to serve all of their wants, needs, and eccentricities. let's contemplate strike a tock okay let's not Aw who cares it's 10 o'clock......and why here I stand stop the clock I need relief to just to walk, let me out! Just another day I have survived this route. Grab my free drink hope it works got so much to do need the perks have a test, think this rehearsal is a dress. Oh I smell through to the pore of south Asian coffee blends I think, I'm not sure....and why am I lost on this dance I need to focus lock everything out optimal performance. Learn to be less human in this race is what they want to set the scene and pace. Have us chasing a dream that's not ours and with no hope of reach I'm lost to what it is we are suppose to teach. People working so hard to spend a coffee dollar, all of them boiling in line, texting, and ready to holler. If I don't look their way, spell their name just the way they say cause goodness forbid someone should take a crack cup literally and it'd be too much to explain oh no the suffering it's clear they forgot that the whole world could be listening the fog of their internal monologue just for the entertaining. Maybe make them forget that their starving can't pay rent, dying all alone going wild needing someone to vent. But we're lost to concepts of quality in the things that really do matter and instead we look for it in silly useless hang-ups that this world makes us deem to matter. Who made them the boss the creators of our universe every man should rule his own keep the flow true and diverse. Believe me things seem to be going much worse. How can we lose touch feels all wrong and things aren't as much of such. 12:00 o'clock walk into class think I can sleep and at the same time pass this test and that test all that is blowing at me maybe your throwing at me in the hallway trying to get your rise Images of trends names of names branded in minds eye all little methods to disguise. Still I persevere strive forward and try. I believe I can fly. 10:10 p.m. I need some sweet shut eye.

6:32 Jump out of bed, found myself hot with cold sweat, no time for a shower, or anything to feed me fuel or power. I think things might be alright, I'll be okay, pull into the lot before the start of the hour. But, we're open and I gotta just stroll right on in and shame walk as those patrons they all ogle me, guys consider we, while the ladies just mentally spit on me; all because they had to come down here and still pick up on the thing that I have created and caused sensations all over their taste buds. Of course it is bomb, it wouldn't be no back shelf duds, and as I maintain my area time space and goods. I let a few shots slide make them high because you know that I could, and would. And everyone is smiling with me Sinatra's on deck serenade; any other morning no one would notice if there dropped a grenade… of loaded whip cream can you leave the lid off? so I can sip cream get it on my lips then lick it off whipped scene. Whoa! Um, was that out loud to the room? Or have I really tried to seal up my doom? With any man or potential gentleman that would have otherwise given thought or his smiles to me, anything to keep rolling on through café insanity. Still a.m. @ 9:23 Only a half hour and some change, I've gotta relax spread out my wings in full range. I look in the mirror, this room seems to flow in my mind much clearer. Think about the facts of life and why they do what they do. That people watch, sit in the back seat, cruise, and analyze; see what they teaching about each other and why the reason to have power and try to say the right words instead of true words tweet-tweet like a song from a song-less bird. 10-to-11:00 a.m. And I got lost again. It's happened twice this week don't know where to begin or rather continue. I've got ten drinks on the bar and the blenders are spinning off in the distance oh I can calibrate set my mind back on reality zip faster catch up to where I should really be. I can do it as long as the flow it keeps on going. Oh my word I think I jinxed myself shouldn't have said a word now a back-up don't take any more orders Please! I can't catch up it's 12:15p.m. I traveled far somewhere in "The Space Between" which in fact that song is playing on in the back-ground for in our lobby the greatest hits can be found and yes I slipped back twice to check on the sound, it's important, but I did in fact get lost, now the guy in line is doubting the quality and cost. Listen man how did I get lost and then oh here comes my back up now we're partnered and both jacked up, wow, as two shots of hot smooth espresso and yes con panna clink of paper as we toast it on the low gotta call out the next drink think it's for Anna. And now the art and coffee flow and the people come in, come out, come in, come out, come in, come out, and finally it's dead there's no crowd, and we play rest and recovery like it all took nothing out of me, shine on the new folks who are entering the room. Don't give them a chance to let eyes linger or begin to loom. Then finally the sealer for the day, a man considers the register his device and open mike and he should say what he say and then he rips us one because in his eyes, we could have never been able to get it all done meet his needs while at the same time the needs of everyone, and he's entitled to his freedom speech ranting and we all hand out samples and ask for the passing, this storms the next storm like all of the others. Then a lady looks over and feels empathy she walked right up to me and then man left us and she said she had to commend us we handled it so well and how I kept up my cool with no giant ordinary tool so now a gift she is giving and our eyes they were glistening, as she spoke of our bravery and choice words I just shivered then in my head she delivered tickets for all of us to go to DisneyLand. "Haha I'M GOING TO DISNEYLAND!!" HEHE I always wanted to say that feel so like Casey step up to bat and the game I've won It's the end of my day on the dot I'm walking on out and the clock says 1:00p.m. Then I'm lifted by as I drive away and I feel so airy lost in Beatle tones of peace and truth I keep in-between the lines and on my face stays a smile just lost in the day I think that word has been the word of the day. I say lost I Sing ~ Lost, ahhhhh I'm content in this day maybe listen to RENT in this day cuz I'm so very lost in this beautiful day and no one can say I didn't live and feel it full so full of happy today. Look how long I've stopped just to make it clear and say. Maybe even sway. Remember for a moment when summer wind came on around 7 I danced the foxtrot with Barista preacher John and it felt like Heaven what brought me back was the thought of changing out pastry trays and fixing the store displays for I would have been lost from that moment still another came and I got lost on that moment and so today has been a lost and wonderful day. Song ends......1:44 I make way up the path and hope I can make it not alone through the door I hope there are others at my timing and state. This teacher will cause a debate and I'll have no other way but to sit through shades of red but I feel blue like Kiss me Kate. Try to make it work and school and try to look like I've been listening follow all of the rules to make it through this lecture pop-quiz, exam, or semester. Whatever the case I have to make it through because they are all counting on me yes I know they're counting on me the ones here with me the ones ahead the ones behind me the ones who got to hear the words I said. The ones so full of truth no question they always understood to the ones that could only know in solemnly time. I wish I could have walked longer with some the ones who showed eager potential the ones with fire and drive in this walk so essential. On this chess board game it's a battlefield where all exists love and a sword to wield to give and still protect your heart you hope you can win from the start and this world tears your heart apart. I can relate to you and I know you feel it through to your core just as you have came through that door you simply wanted to know more. Our eyes and energies collide and we both hope to realize that there is no co-incidence we're here to feel this experience and in all moments live in truth and fruitful spirit declare the love in which we share. This world makes so many rough spots on our hearts and minds makes us believe we can never find love and even if we do it won't last and even trying will hurt too. I don't know what to tell you, but I love you like you are my brother and I love you like no one other for you are you and I could never mistake you for you are you and I have lived here in these moments with you. 6:37 p.m. time for dinner cook for just me it isn't easy. Zone off and get lost yes I said lost in the music and a playlist or 3 later I get down on my knees and I say good night and prayers express my hopes and fears if I sit too long I'll have to wipe up my tears then I slide on to the cool crisp linen on the bed. I brush my hair back fit a spot on my pillow for my head and I dream as I do every night and I look once more at the ticking on clock how did I lose 4 hours on classic rock. Yawn and close eyes and midnight 12:00 o'clock.

Chapter 3: Day 3

"RING RING RING" Jump up like it's a three ring I think I hear the circus as I shower music plays this morning I feel just like a flower on the box of this soap I'm happy with my choice now this scent is so dope it's true the graphic didn't capture me from the beginning and why am I fixed on this the showers over last cereal bites as I try to pass this Rover need the fast lane and this trip over. "Man how did I get Here!" I woke up early had time makes no sense this isn't clear. Think this is all too much and I'm losing the grasp even the touch pull it together as I lock the door and walk away and into the den of lions Ha I wasn't late again and I grin at Ralph oh Mr 50 old Ralph and he grins back with sin for he knows I'm not late again. I clock it in with time to spare and I get a chance to tie up my hair and do my deep breaths of energy setting for this shift is gonna zip by is what I'm betting and there shall be no major issues and everyone will be not wanting to misuse just wait and see step up to the register sign in at 11:03. I got marker on my hand no big deal here I stand as I try and wipe of the black stripes and here comes the crowd a hundred all different types with their different to be different and here comes number 1 test me I'm patient as you don't even look at me like I'm not here and why would I be and I say this not for me but for the ones who are standing still in this moments they look to you and you don' show them the human in your humanity instead spread i-phony insanity i-me and i-want i-coffee. How did you lose touch I don't smile because I'm unhappy but I don't smile because it hurts me that you can be right here and yet so far from me and you think that reality is what you see. I wish I could share really what it is to be free and to live free believe before you see not see before you believe. And I am singing in my head through my day I penciled a few lines down and played it forward here in this town as I sit here and collect all my thoughts and bring the words together like a concoction a mixture all the right ingredients this soy chai is pure and simple brilliance I sip nutmeg on my senses as I trip tip-toe up to the register and I stand ready for the next one and the next ones here I stand and the clock has a few tick-tocks past 1:00 Todays chaos seems like a battlefield I can function in this battlefield and every so often a smile comes through and touches my soul and I carry on because I know there is hope and there is something worth it all as I strive through the wasteland I keep my eyes through the waste of land and today I feel Love in the distance. I always feel it off in the distance when my heart and soul are at their most connected points it's a beautiful instance I can hear my love call over the shores and I wish I could bring us closer for more and then I come back to cold reality. How this world makes it hard to find the thing that is true and real and still has me baffled at what two people can truly feel. 3:06 p.m. I have given a 60-second tutorial on the syrups and process by which we add more or less to the drinks depending on the size and overly simplified the data in hopes that I could help was helpful to realize. The man still looks at me with puzzlement like the information was suppose to add some sort of clarity to his decision making and the understanding over our menu and disparity now he throws his money down like he hates the thought of charity. He pushes his glasses up while two women behind him tap their feet but not too hard as they adjust their matching nose-job wraps because they think I noticed even at the first toe tap. Like I didn't notice, like no one could, help but see the typical stay at home hood, mom in this city of smoggy-fog visual validity. So hard to keep them straight make them not hate for the call that they made wasn't right on the day. "Dry Cappuccino!" How did I end up this long on the bar, where did my friend go, this was supposed to only be a break, where in beans burning is he how long will he take. I'm getting worried… I'm not stocked… I'm running low… and I can't go I'm stuck in this cold front of blending and ice show. Now the guys and girls who look like extras of the OC peer down their rhino plastery and stare at me like they shouldn't be waiting but I'm too ignorant for the debating and I can't hear their loud and obvious remarks for in some weird language anyway I would bark and I roll my eyes and throw lids and wipe ill-pouring away pass out straws and make them walk themselves away. They look like dragons with green straws up their nose and I dish pity in their cups like a peace rose for they know not of the world they speak like fools of knowing all and bending rules with a name or a dollar while they crack the vile take what makes not bi-polar and pull up on their collar for they know no other way they've grown up to hear listen what they say and they follow with ears follow slip into empire fooled to think you lead but yes you do follow. What they do to be untouchable but wanted why do people confuse and raise an attitude and cannot forgive don't they know together we all live and it means all the world your thoughts your wins your inside out and the things that have to be said aloud. 3:03p.m. It's time to go stop this thinking don't let it show gotta call home and hope they don't hear my pain through the call. I miss them so and can't believe how I let the last two weeks just go. Like time flew as if I had fun believe struggle and stress time runs and I'm writing and finishing the last report 12:52 a.m. I can sleep I'll be just fine if I set the alarm and remember time. Think I forgot to take out these contacts oh me……yawn, crash, and zzzzzzzzzzzzzz.

Chapter 4: Day 4

"Whoa! How did I get here?" I seriously can't remember waking up or getting ready got to hold on to the wheel and steer. Clock says 4:43a.m. and you feel the sharp pain of where time usually runs you through in the back, take a step away yoga breaths and relax, you're on time gonna be alright a good day mmmm maybe today will be a good tip day Ugh! I hate to think of money this place speeds up your thoughts of money always flash and fame designed for you designed so out on a stick and you watch as they dangle hypnotize with good angles and you're sold just like the rest and in the wrong you invest so you can always have a method to blame and think that flawless is the way you will search but above this there is a way that makes it gold if you could just kiss the stubborn away and feel free the way the one and only way. 8:00 a.m. and why did I even look up I should know better by now to have loaded like three hundred more cups. Everyone's on the phone and I swear and want to bust out mine even break and get my tooth blue so I could work double time. Here she comes she steps up and orders a troop of drinks twenty-two and still wants personal names and to teach the room to spell all of them too. And I smile like Hollywood and zombies stood there in front of me lost in my eyes and colors I chose that day. 99 and 100 were very sweet tall Z's time lingered for a minute and soaked in as I just breathed and then it all went back like a remix and the next two hours the same patterns begin to flow from the guy who just doesn't know to the girls who giggle in like on crack 8 shots of espresso with 8 sugars over ice in venti-cup this is how they started their night on the up. Most worked through

Pas to the Ocean strip clubs and service lines all there to give you some motion. To order this at this time you know they funked their business strategy and they're ignoring all possible signs that say sleep. Serving crazy 88's I'll always remember blonds with snow like mid-december blood shot eyes but in designer disguise they can hide their pain and personal identity to be the something that they think that someone else wants to see. 10:54 a.m. Been pretty good so far things have kept their distance but I do feel bad for my associates they had their day we all go through it when there just is nothing we can say. The storms come in and take a weathering on us and it teaches of life and people and you step back and see them get so wrapped and not like bubbles in the sense of light and happy but in the way that they're cold wet and sappy they're so quick to cut and run. I had a girl come to me here at 11:13a.m. and bringing questions high to a sight we both could touch and asked for my fellowship on such what made her suffer on this sunny day??.. I told her I'm glad she looked my way, and she knew that within her answers to the questions there was a way, and in minutes we spoke in volumes beyond just one wave-length, could have measure if sounds and motions of our speech were silver threads and jeweled treasure you'd be amazed by view and you would know what in this world was true and not be blind to the show of what is screened. Their all wired can't win and we serve up the brew milk in the tin and connect still with living souls and not ones lost into their roles. 1:00 p.m. and I walk the line as Cash sings and exit as Ring of Fire comes to it's coda portion of the song I'm off tomorrow and the next but I know it won't feel so long as it creeps up on my happy parade of freedom and sanity like a fog in northern cali bays to mellow out my day. 1:47 p.m. I switch up the gears to make it up the hill my way and around the bend and then I back again at this school another day repeat walking along up this lonely cold street as I place a beat on my life and heart spend moments longing that someone would be touched and make a fresh start. Am I causing down a path of lost hopes think the coffee has me buzzing and high on thoughts and walking tight ropes. Who am I entertaining who sees is it the angels with me or the ones who think they see it all do they watch would they interact and save me if I fall. I've got no net just how I like it and I've even placed a bet on my own philosophy and way of art to be I hope when the time comes he really does see me and not want this world tries to make of me. What I want I wish I could etch in stone and wear on my chest so that all would know how clear my thoughts and wants are truly. Never could be so simple that's silly and even if it could work to my plan the probability is that no one would read it anyway and it'd be my lot to tote my weight and then I wouldn't be so free from the bearing constraints unable to color my tapestries with illuminating paints. Ahhh Art class at 04:45 p.m. fifteen more minutes and I'll be flying out of here past them. Thoughts of dinner and cooking a feast I'm so hungry could eat like a beast. I walk out of school and hop in the car begin to drive and I run into 134 hell and wonder at the source of this traffic is someone still alive. The numbers and MPH show serious severity and all are patient that roll with me no horns or fighting we just go on in peace, and the sun sinks even lower while reds and purples fill the air. The regal colors soar over head for all to share and the warmth leaves the sky The pace it begins to pick up and they engines let lose and rev up and we spread to the wind again. All of us trying to make it home and recover our fire and wind so that tomorrow we may burn again. 6:30 p.m. Sat in the car for an extra ten minutes as the song on the dial has me contemplate a while of love and this world of sin will I ever win or have my love so dear and if it were here would I have the eyes to know that it is the one so clear? A light dinner by the light of a candle for tonight I feel the regular bright light is too much too handle I would rather have the romance glow so I can drift off and dream so so of my coming true of what I long and wish I'm so sick of everyone talking about people like fish for this isn't a sport or a game it's a way of life in a personal frame. 11:02 and I've got nothing to do but enjoy out my night and carry on the delight but it's taken so much out of me and I feel so eyes heavy and sleep can someone tell me a story and fable with some morals and lay it all on the table my fantasy and dream hit the button and enable…..I'll sleep slip into dreams….I'll sleep slip into dreams. REM hit me but not the group please give me an oasis of story away from real and this place give me some peace so I can wear it like a mask protect from each punch to the face.

3:30p.m.There aren't that many names I've written from thin air, still there have been some great and others like oh no contraire. A question every now and then how and why I was able to scribe before word, I explain as best I heard send them on their way hold no curd. Almond Mocha keeps on talking even spelling as his name is scribed ink drying all the while he is still deciding finally looks to see if you heard the last letter hoping this drink and tart makes his day better. Send him down past the others as he wonders why his way I don't spy. We are 2 in the hole and the line to the door is extending past hours, six jugs in hand as I reset hope everything in place we can withstand the blowback of angry people loaded phone in hand strained eyes look we can't deliver. Clergy from down the street should be in soon don't forget all their extra sugars and spoons. One store on the edge of oblivion ran by fools who keep mold and tragedy in their brew and hope their cold doesn't ring true. Sirens blare sirens eyes see all the pain the homeless man cries, the lost, the hoping to be seen todays new wave hooligan or street queens. At least it's not a parade of roses with end of the world barrels of fire. Reminds me of when I gave bags of pastries the trash would have eaten to a room full of souls whose lives humanity has been mistreatin'. Only a couple look up but I don't need a thanks I just knew the right thing to do even though it was against the ranks. People and systems make it hard to maneuver when others need help I can still see the faces the hungry the tired the empty who show up to help our store came across the valley and popped up through a magical door. This city makes us all suffer to work, suffer to play, suffer to learn the wages of everyday in the city of angels and airbrush fantasies. Sometimes covered in sweat and coffee I drive towards the sun drift off in the tones of sublime and subliminal fun. Each day a different journey a possible quest or original disaster. LBC always there as I sit an empty house with no pastor. Hummingbirds signal the peace and ability to recharge. A quiet moment a distant thought reminding me of the life so far I have bought. Do we continue do we change or is this some other world always on the brink of strange. Gotta refuel I pull in the pumps are down I circle back puff clouds turn it up and roll these wheels past clowns. Up and down the boulevard so many out and about energy not even taxed like they've been working off my back but I know I'm just out of gas and fumes need to relax. I keep the radio up and hope it doesn't play something from our selection in the lobby now I know I need a change new job or maybe just a hobby. American beauty came in made every man grin with sun. A doe is what I saw bright eyed and strong. I looked down the bar and made sure her drink wasn't off or waiting to long. Some people are too sweet and their demands are never harsh and often a treat. She didn't have change so we didn't stress and on her way we sent her all blessed and cup in hand. As Tony sang against the band the time went tick today I didn't want to carry a big a stick. Humbly serving optimistic to kindness and others lacking in need knowing there are so many who strive but really need a good deed. When times are easy or clarity is true things within reason like a white ball to the cue. Sink it or swim room full of sharks day or night I struggle from my depths to fend of their fight. Like anyone momentous pursuing their path it takes a lot for me to stop and echo wrath. I'm not here to be stepped on or held down for the next I walk tall and save others from the drown. Keep your head up and keep moving find your flow even when others tell you how to move walk talk and flow. Each decade against the next soul perplexed to be awakened asleep is easier to couple with vex. Croissants and green tea seem clean and something I need to feed me. I mix a

perfect cup sit back and forget about tax let the death of
the last drop let me savor it to the max. Cinnamon and
passion fill the air how can there be any room for despair
I mow our breed is rare humans all wanting somewhere
to go and stare. More than half able to create art or matter
instead of useless lies and chatter. I left the medical walk
in hopes to rock the talk inspire hope and increase
audible range now I sling espresso and count back
change. How can this be efforts towards a life of
impassioned pursuit I'm convinced it's never been about
the dress or suit. 12:04a.m. Walking to the car paid more
for parking then we did at the bar. Still I almost met Neo
he came into the room like a Leo. Kate and I stood up in
awe and I forgot to relax and moved across the room raw.
Did saps read into a wall a room full of eyes wouldn't
answer my call. I know it was true and I missed my boat
he came through the hall to the seat where I sat but I
didn't leave a note. The singer sang and the strings filled
the room and the bittersweet moment hung in the loom.
Sunset walks and music filled nights I dreamed I would
find such delights. Far from home no locals tonight
seems like we all came for the glow just to get closer to
light. 2:09a.m. Hours from event horizon and a blast
from the sun how is it that my rest hasn't even begun.
Schedules against reason just to test reminds you of
numbers and how to excel and be above the mess. This is
temporary this shall pass, don't invest more time than
you have to last. Sleep, sleep, and not a chance. I try to
dial as I look up at the time for one last glance the phone
is too close for romance.

Chapter 6: Day 6

Fifteen pounds is what they say the average coffee clerk gains just from working here. Depressing yet so true I remember when it was time to go and I wouldn't need a buzz or starting your shift with a drink just cuz. A pastry a simple pleasure paired with a decadent bold brews something that's meant for me and not for you. Decadent chocolate and whip cream fill the air everyone orders like your waist has nothing to care. In this city you know it's a lie like the girl coming cross the tracks needs her cup to work optimal performer she dance and makes her way every night. Those shots almost 10 buzz her into the beyond she forgets she spent a quarters wage on a slow night. It starts again the push and uphill we go this time I'm sick and before I can start from a break my stomach has some notes I need to take. I'm told to leave and I take the awkward advice I speed on home before the round ends these dice. I stop side of the freeway in one of the largest and busiest around. Six months with the noise and bustle I admit I never was one to hustle.

I'm a zen warrior a keeper and seeker of the stars. I humbly serve and help those that need help seems to be everyday. This world will kill you if you let it a friend says across the quiet one as we reminisce. Friends so close but distances so great o never find that one guy to kiss. I rise with night when I feel my soul fight and I rise with the dawn when I feel I can't go on. The spirit in me stirs with the tides, moon, and stars; we cruise through the universe like a parade of old school cars. Thinking of quitting, moving store, or a move in between cleaning the grit and grime all stuck in the groove. Refrigerator coils are simply the worst, women and children their counts of bacteria in league with death disburse. Each day we seem to do so much more but it only feels like it's gotten worse. There's no outdoor vents or way for us to exit trash so through the main door we go with shame and hopes no eyes show dread. Complaints within the core aren't allowed and you're problem if you say. If it's known this has been done you'll count every last day. They took some down to their bunker and made up lies, all for glory, coffee, and devil with no care or cries. What is this madness of elite thinking with fast food motion. On the surface so adorned yet slimed with moldy commotion. This is not conducive to my goals and who I want to be they say benefits and the name are only part of making you bigger in this game. I miss the meetings and the team building to inspire us for change, but like any preserved thing any new growth is strange. Where do I go with this extra weight and experience. Who would want a coffee employee with no perks or what they call a burnt bean. Where would newness afford me an opportunity to use the skills and abilities I possess while letting me heal from the corporate beating and group humiliation for my pay. Is this what goes on for 2 weeks just to get my pay? There's gotta be a better solutions a road a bypass or paved entry level way, quick c'mon before more of my brain is lost on this decay.

3:30 a.m. woke up like bad clock-work and I think on again where did the last two days go and why is that thing I remember coming up in my mind too slow. I think it was a good day at work where did the last two days go feel like I was robbed by a jerk…..drift off for ten minutes for a little more sleep now it's 4:00 o'clock and I'm jumping again no time to weep 4:26 a.m. "I have to keep my hair long for a part I'm committed to and now I take long in trying to just work with my do gotta wear this hat puts me in the mood to step up to bat and be a winner and some days I just hide under the bill with my smile and I can feel them try and take a look under they wanna steal some of my thunder and powerful energy on this day and still not remember me I won't have it this way not today or any other day. In the nick of time chasing dreams and facing deadlines the right things come as the wrong things go keep my eyes open so i can follow the show stand next to the blind and ask them why cause them to think n question inside so many walks of people all looking to still be able to read through to the inside. Hoping to keep their instincts for this world we are in although they know this that their motives are sick and have changed a bit I know right forbid but what you seek aren't compatible and you question what is not palatable and refuse to swallow what you can't explain. Some things don't have such a square rooted answer or writable presence, but an unexplained trait that at least is clear make no mistake. Five minutes to 7:00 and in strolls Mr slice of Heaven a tall dark and dreamy statue that smiles and says I'll protect you from this cold hard world and keep you safe and warm girl but it's just flirty silly nonsense no different you think that I would have had sense than to let him stimulate my mood again place on line as a ten. It's gotta be too good to be true He has a Mrs. Or girl at home they always do…think they would come up with a better story maybe that's why I haven't asked to hear his story because he'd make it sound original and true they always do. City of Angels where no men stand and here they come to be charged and typed by their brew. I can call out the personalities by the order taste and what consider please what they do to them they crave and stumble to call out. This is what I like but I have trouble to say like an expression of doubt. Like when I ask what your tuned into on your iPod and you can't say like I should not have gave away prod to interact with you. Don't hide off in your world let me discover you like we are one boy and one girl. I think I got side-tracked by Mr. Almond Latte I still often wonder what he thinks I've got to say would he ever walk in and make my day. 9:16 a.m. and we've sold every pastry in sight the fearless leader is ranting and we try to hide shades of delight. Then I 'm cleaning my station and then a smell a subtle creation begins to linger and call to me hypnotically….with earthy warmth and floral notes to give me pleasure I'm taken away on a voyage so deep I cannot measure where I have gone or from where I come under the sun and this flavor I inhale and take in makes me feel like I'm home and the island I feel deep within. Maybe Sumatra or another isle deep within organic shade grown with scent so mmmm bold off it's land so far away it has taken me away. I'm set now on automatic serving up all I can hear is static but I respond like second nature and I create foam such rich creamy foam for two double tall caps and a dry 20 decaf on the way so many shots pour and finally it spawns on me a problem needing called the beast who is refusing to satisfy the needs everyone one inside on this all of a sudden rainy day and the music is turning weird for the most part I think I gotta run a new playlist I must start here in this minute at a minute past 12:00 p.m. I walk away from it and then I feel the crowd turn like I wronged them. Have

to set my flow and take over the reigns of this show
churn out the energy smooth like butter make all of them
drop thoughts of revenge on me. They're getting what
they came for and they received much more for I've been
spiking adding extra and enticing only a couple heads
complained because a shot extra of sugar is too much and
they are sensitive and need it delivered as such so I
remade but it didn't dampen my day. These rolling stones
help to keep me solid and strong been alone for so long
and on this song my focus is gone then for a second feel
so spun make it end. Then the crowd dies down and the
sunset is passed and people get calm from the first to the
last and it's so peaceful and we can finally see the
condiment bar. All tore up in shambles a bot steps up and
we deploy the star for recovery and I'm lost watching
this star cuz he shines so bright for he carries the light
like a torch bearer. Oh me 2:03 does anyone know whose
suppose to be relief the villagers are restless in line ready
to pitch fork us like beef.

04:30 a.m. Bright red and loud in my ear started out fuzzy but now it's getting clear, reach to hit the snooze button but my other hand wants to steer so I turn it off and put the futon up and away think I gotta get up or maybe get fifteen either way. Morning time in pictures, as still as a statue, white lights as the faucet spins slide soap bubbles on the tattoo. These Coffee blessed Jordans stick to the pedals as I switch up gears, traffic flow mirror check as this love song brings out tears. Pass the rose bowl and the suns colors flood then hues from wildflowers dawn mountains of green and mud. Ahhh and life is beautiful it's just ones of those days how the world rolls in many ways always creating, causing, and affecting reaction off reaction chemical compound con-fraction. 5:10 and the gas light is begging me when I'm snapped out if and now my tears have switched to now from then. Then it makes me laugh how simple and silly my struggle among all this worlds real issue then I searched the glove for a tissue found a napkin now look what happen I just rolled right on through a light they also took a picture so there's no chance for a fight. Now I turn up sublime and I just get lost for one last time a few cool blocks accompanied by this beat with rhyme. Weekly search for the key card then wait found it in record speed few other employees pull in and then I rush to make the lead. Speed walk below the level of looking silly, kinda waist down warms you up makes you forget how dark and chilly, life and this moment really is as the city lies lifeless and stoney hmmm maybe for lunch sup with macaroni, keys twist, reaches for the lights clock in run to the alarm oops can't win the signal went off now expect a call carry on brew the coffee and tea ready ice, fight not to eat the pastry. The crew always spoke of the Infamous 10…..solid pounds of gain-age once your crew. Expect you'll get it sooner than the end. Some days you just give in right away so it gets you through like a stiff drink of glazed confection go to a happy place like they all seem to do. The eclectic coffee social café wheel spinning everything from the music to the pupils of your eyes with the off rhythm of your heart. You take a doppio shot light foam to the head and then all of a sudden you remember what last zombie said. He was the informer the one who came to speak to me of milk. He pushed up his glasses and jiggled the milk craft in front of me in case I didn't' speak English or was a sufferer of headphone implant deafness. Then fast forward to this moment look around and know that we pay rent so I oblige the restless crowd make my way and go mission out to the far rings beyond our counter and pick-up station to the dreaded and battle endured condiment bar……I am remembering at this walk of the long standing idea that I would never work around food in reality it should have been not to work around people that are rude.0916 a.m. Deep breaths and tranquil thoughts surround me as I slowly come back to this waking life and the 16th minute of my 15 minute brake Of course they're watching the clock for goodness sake and I stretch am awake take two steps and feel the ache in my shoes for I've been standing too long and those silly waffle mats don't help instead they hinder as we try not to collide in our box as the people watch and we watch them. Then the crowd rushes us and we gasp try to relax and the ticking begins like a bomb with no shelter explode from within I saw that man felt her and he got away just another sick guy trying to liven his day. Sheesh and that ain't the way stepping on each other pushing the line in front of you because you've got two minutes to what needed to be done in ten and now you raise your voice to the high and mighty heavens. Well we're not you're witness at 7-11 and I'm so lost in

madness that I'm forgetting my class I'm late guess these
two guys stepping up a chance I'll never date because
I gotta fly on out of here like it's the moment I've been
waiting for and will I learn or will my spirit always need
to feel this pace and speed. Now the lecture is turning
grey and I rub my eyes and try not to fade away.

"Wake up!" and feel just fine still dark and I sing like a lark and hope the neighbors they don't hear or raise hell I think I sound sweeter than the sound of a bell. Really? You think they would care more for the alarm than the quality voltage of my piping charm. Heehee and I'm cheery so madly like sweet dreams came and they had me oh yes it's true at 4:32. Time enough for hair and make-up I carry on like I wear no wake-up and breakfast things call from out the door and around the bend wish there was a clone I could send. Oh well steps to kitchen toss and fire heat simmer the sustenance which will soon begin my very day and the day of all those zombies. They'll stroll right in and order a werewolf change and act all good like it's not all off the wall and strange. I put on the bill keep up with the drill that is this soldiers walk and live like free will not lost in conformity for the form of me is coming across you and as you step into my light try not to resist don't try to put up the fight for my drinks they will spin and cause of you blissful coupage de sol. 5:40 the car is a lock and I walk in like I've got no connection to clock and what is selling all I know is today's stories and what they're telling it's on the face of society deep in the quadrants of Angels city. They think that I do not see but there are others just like me who see you when no one sees you and you should care because it's true that even you see you and you are part of something bigger than the universe....across the universe echoes deep inside as I place on my skin the armor like a hide. I step out and its loud the café is filled with multiple orders sliding at the bar let loose out the gate 3 caps, Iced teas, and chocolatey freeze no pauses to check the price or the rate. The men, women, and zombies all throw bills, and we all roll sleeves grit teeth and show skills. The craft how it brings them such pleasure all earth tones of dark to light sprinkles and sugar sparkle like edible treasure. Of course a faux-gent zombie steps up and asks "Sweetie talk about your treats" I look back at the case which is filled with butters and sweets ignore because there is no time to stop on his lousy cold dime. Ugh! The ones so creepy who prey in on such moments, and still come to ones who see them through the chaos of what is going on. They know the zombies don't see, can you imagine even officer zombie not far off can't see the energy the ill thrive on his intent. Then he moves on and peers like a Tom who doesn't have to peep, because this Babylon makes it too easy like a cake he just has to take and you hear it every day. You know there are so many other ways and this could not exist like snow in May in walls of this city. I take a five not fifteen to regain my strength and stretch out my pain from sore sleeping and too many hours this a.m. at the bar. 09:45 and I am back on-line serving them left and right bringing foam to a frothy delight I whip stir and build on it and pour the loaded shot glasses over the rich creamy foam and the chocolate toned liquid decides with the foam on such a hue you hear Elvis and think of a beach with palms surrounded by blue. I am the queen of foam and cream I like to let the artist shine and thrive know that in two seconds when it's destroyed it touches your heart so alive. The mix into your blood and through your veins you wish this to flow. Suck through the straw like fangs need it to go isn't this strange and people can be scared of vampires…..and still why can't they see these zombies guess you have to work here or know with whom you pledge. Iced coffee which cause of complains morphed like a caterpillar to a butterfly oh the tracks change and they sing of the jasmine in my mind and I'm lifted again up and out of this place then I touch back down and sign on again into the human race. Touched back down in middle of a rush this I I'm taking orders playing middle man and energy lock master I

write like hell I tag the cups shake groove twist turn and
move faster. There are way too many drinks hanging out
on top of the twin beasts now I slide yay! Go me to
the aide and we shut it down like Macy's parade we are
the coffee fronts of this brigade and we show no
expression and so embedded lost in our task at hand I
pump pump opps! Because of my height I get a big shot
of taste two pumps of vanilla fly into mouth 11:10a.m.
from a back fire off some invisible wall and ponder and
my mind begins to wander possibly from the sugar rush
held inside on my tough do I spit it out or swallow or
should I to the restroom do run. Then like a change I
swallow it down and get my job done. A few grins from
the audience of on-lookers concerned with their drink.
A fashionista looking metro tells me nicely, "I think
my drink is missing a couple shots dear." I slightly blaze
red and to behind the beast I choose to steer. Then the
drinks they build upon the bar and Frank, John, and
Sharon are lost in café cell-phone-I and have 10-minute
drinks standing solo cup like a kids with no ride after
school still looking for someone to pick them up. Then
one by one the trio walk and one by one they pick up
their drink, and I cringe in hopes I don't have to look up
or think….but I should have at least twenty minutes, and
now since I've stayed to give my aide now I stand to face
possibly the firing squad like a swimmer sinking their
wade all cuz I'm late to the clock to stop my time card's
tick tock…can't win is this some sort of sick sin now the
clock strikes 12:20 and I'm stuck in the mode of can't
win. Shake it off and hope something plays well on the
waves and the DJ's aren't stuck on midday sappy songs,
or group therapy sessions all the stations locked in like
they are all in conference and the sounds come across
like a shock wave of picket fence and I forgot to bring
my music today, so I'm left to their mercy and hope
it's sweet mercy, cuz I need a friend or hand even if it's
on the other end of this fm band.

Chapter 10: Day 10

11:47a.m. I've slept in and can't begin to think of my day. The eyes just close, and thoughts start to fade. A memory of the dreams I just dreamt of the pillow and the way it felt, and now I've got to adjust twist and turn. Ow! Oh! I must for my joints I don't want to rust. Am I thinking too out loud? Standing in class naked, maybe flying, or dreaming of love of being underwater and holding on tight to a kiss, no need for air I can handle this, and a little bit more if there is more to have and see in-store, on the horizon as the mirages they dance to intercede, shifty stick out sore to the sight like a run in my gartered with heels high tight. Then I'm standing on stage and the spotlight comes back on from a fade, and there's a flower in my hair; take a breath and leap off like freedom in the bird whose caged like if this scene was a page, and a story you sought was to unfold like honey and cream a taste to be told. Sensations now I'm hungry wanted more sleep now body doesn't agree with me and I must leave dreams and wake walk and daydreams I must settle for till next slumbers taunts and soothing unconscious mind's eye sees an adventure or passage into a sweet dream then again I take cake over moon walk. Rude awake, but bittersweet for the birds haven't given out once a sign or tweet. I can stay in mellow mode like sandals and ripped up jeans walking down a country road. Days gone by and times once passed was it all real or are they memories at the end of the day delivered last like the mail man's lazy and I'm the house he's passed. Carry to bear, bear to carry grab up the reigns of the moments in life, my moments and the ones at hand here in order ready to nobly stand. This I, my beating hearts demand just as you can see as it sits here on the sleeve like tattoo unseen to all as every beat has hit the walls as solid as a rock in times when self force of the wall couldn't even stand the structure held strong and tight. The river of red always in circulation flood water rotation, keep my pulse up and regulate to keep me healthy alive and good spirits state. 02:15 p.m. Cross the street step up steps to post now to market maybe search for something to roast. Why roast is my conscious sub telling me to live life hold the glass high and toast? Hours past middy and all I see is the post still unopened but at least it's on this side of the door maybe there's good news I should read make the life in me want more. I think then wait hold on here am I getting lost in an industrial force field am I to my pick ax and grab with grip to wield? Today is the off day the beginning of a 2 in a row free day, no thoughts of tools, work or schools rules I should be like a bird carefree and sail. Stroll to the movies or pack up to the beach. Find the hidden life meanings only the wisest would teach. A day oh my day then I look down to comprehend my own realization of the days portions lost to silly rest and sleep. My vice my dark cave the card up my sleeve. Lost in dreams and maybe meaningful messages I turn over as the sun tries to creep through the blinds and I feel my heartbeat and the pulse carries a message to remind I am alive. I tug and pull the covers and wrap them with one leg. Then drift off in late afternoon daydreams as the scent of my hot chocolate lingers all over the room with the dash of vanilla in the scoop of ice cream that took whips place. Oh how the chocolate did sooth to set my smile and pace. 07:47 and the sun has set the cool night air rolls in and tickles my eyelashes to stir my still eyes. Though in dreams I react and still jump to surprise. Is it night is it day am I fired do I work today? Come back around and gather my reigns then attempt to charge my phone and rejuvenate the power veins. Boil a kettle for tea and possibly a simple treat to accompany my worn books a wasteland of a genius' retreat. My glasses in exchange for two invasive disks of sight provide a much more even sooth to compliment and complete my night.

Chapter 11: Day 11

      The days begin to blend like the sound of the mixers never stopping your whole shift. Gallons of perfected sweet liquids pour down the drain ready for the next order and list at least we have no lemons to twist and today I've got a pale shadow of where time would sit on my wrist. I realize it's past time for a break just because I don't smoke cigarettes they think I'll forget and make the mistake. I look up and see Mr. Reynolds standing by watching me craft, organize chaos, and serve zen on the side. Venti Vanilla Latte I call out Ryan with the hazel blue eyes. I step back and turn cold play on it's the X and Y for the last few drinks I take in the hot late summer air and let my mind stroll through fields of thinks. Am I where I'm supposed to be or did I miss the bus. Is there something more I should be doing than just letting go and trust. Any other day passed the suicide bridge not looking at everyone looking at the pretty lights. A Romantic scene so many spent lost with self fight. The street named like a river flows all through the stretches of the limits. You can't help but take it in and feel all it's trials and triumphs, it's somber energy calling your soul.

      Iambic pentameter and structure haunt my waking day dreams and nights of mental cataloguing. I've got the beat and dig the flowery flowetry Shakespeare did pen, I admit William had been a hero a purveyor of humanity and love and how to have zen. Unbeknownst to us he toils in his given time as so many homes hold a book, a film, a treasure of his writing. Time is a funny thing and

the words that fill the spaces ring truth bright between to
bring us understanding of people, time, and places. I'm
convinced Keanu, Shatner and Christopher all take time
to tell us more through the beat of their word. Their
choices of poised time to measure adorn the space unlike
any other to some like alphabet treasure. To others they
laugh and make fun deflect abilities of reception it's
easier to poke fun than question. "Can I go home?" I ask
and stand because I've waited for a reasonable place or
break. I convey I've got only hours to sleep and maybe I
made a mistake. Miss Melissa says "oh my gosh, yes
please go home." So the Apothecary fleas the scene of
Romeo and Juliet to climb the stairs and find the car or
was it bed so much chatter and noise not sure if I can
quiet the head. Cotton in my face head and ears echo the
days remarks I'm hoping the bush outside on the street
doesn't ring in hours with a family full of larks. The suns
up I'm late and forgot to set a reminder to time 3 alarms
and snooze I can't think of how to make the alarm louder
or closer to where I go. My sleep my solace fortress of
solitude the place where I consider the day alter the path
and incorporate the way the flow the journey what's now.
Ticket stubs and single lunches around the city become
what lately my mind craves I thought it would be the
sand sun and and Paradise Cove waves. I think of the
solider building the castle across from our store the
charm of a knight I didn't have courage to question to
learn so much more. I a gentleman and hero forever in
my head. A girl lost on a man quest and errand of merit
needed the sword of a king and the inscription he did
scratch and bear it. So much honor on Spanish steel this
queen remembers the feel the gift that one soul gave on
Christmas one day would forever leave a mark deeper
than cuts on the minute notches of a barista's day. $100
dollars a month and storage took the sword a little girl
carrying lost more than her surfboard. Running so lean I
can't go too long without a crunch heaven help the date
that doesn't have a plan of r can't decide to order lunch.
Running all over the city with Shade-Grown ringing
through my head as the summer sun scorched my head,

heart, and spirit. I need a nap us young people don't realize we need rest for the growth until 25 we gotta do and take the most. Wake up and forget did I work tomorrow today or yesterday how is it that I can't see the date or hear anything but orders in my head. All I want is a three day weekend so I can sleep in. I hate to take a vacation or sick day just to rest, aren't we supposed to be out there living our best? Am or fm? where's my band? Where's my contract asking signature? where my microphone hand? Creators lost in a world that won't schedule time to let us create. Like generations before maybe we've lost enough touch that's why no one can antiquate. Preoccupied yet nothing is more than we can take and stress so why make the mistake. I'm supposed to go hear and see David Lynch yet I look at the ticket and the date it's passed with a flinch. I haven't even watched his catalogue so maybe I'm early and should take the time to compute before I ask or shake a moment and seem like a mute. How do I get to the conversations and the tables that make the movements I dream and hope to join fate; all I can do is sit in the planets green room and wait. Do I have a number, are they calling any, or has the moment past I sit back and hear crystal clear Jefferson starship telling of Alice's past. Neo where are you and that white rabbit and pill the caterpillar with the mushrooms hands me choices and tells me I have free will. 11:11p.m. 30 minutes in… a screensaver invades the room jumping off the screen I sit atop the mountainous couch a little forest fairy queen. Everything melts like the whip cream on the drinks not picked off the bar, I run five miles like Fontaine can't touch me, sink into the car leave the radio down. Sit back in my life with the carefree of a clown another cup another pot another day in the volcano parking lot.

Chapter 12:Day 12

04:40a.m. Folded the futon down for the last twenty minutes of heaven flipped my pillow and checked for the snooze should come on at seven I haven't had such a late wake on a work day in I can't remember and why couldn't it have been on a chiller day like last December? I mixed up the shower handles like I was on the other side I stepped through my reflection and I'm living in a tinted mirror. How many days have I been like this? How many times will I swing and miss? That piano of moonlight sonata gotta stop its tones stirring thoughts in my head. I just gotta keep on this path because in a time not too far back I made a path and I said this was the surest path. Now as the coffee wakes me up as I've stood here at the bar don't remember walking in or even locking up the car…and now I'm strolling on a fifteen hoping I don't look like some worried queen all dolled still and comprised gazers buy lost in the soup try to make contact with my eyes. I feel like an alien in one of those films they seek to configure me in the library of their minds. They just can't consider me for all too long something carries their focus away and I look for my out my way. I didn't lock the car but thank God no one came to come up off my mess this a.m. I pull my hat down and I shoot for a nap have the alarm set so I should feel fret. I drift off in dreams and begin to take part Then a short gasp of air just before I swallowed my heart. The alarm was now buzzing in at snooze three…..the time now stood at 6 minutes past 3….or is it 3 minutes past six….oh that sounds much more like it glad it could fix with minimal effort I've got tests up today. I'm ready I'm

tired don't know any other way. It's 6:08 The lines have
formed and they're far from straight, today is play school
day which calls for slower speech and arm gestures
similar to charades to keep these ones at bay…..we make
a suggestion then take their money and they grab their
cup all full of sunny or is it sun-dried….mmmm I could
really deal with some sun-dried exposure I need a
getaway a smooth release then maybe this ground will
sprout peace. Why am I ever trying to change things or
think that the waves and frequencies matter ah because
I'm a dreamer devoted and convicted and the beat of my
heart sounds off my march. 10:15 am.. Fifteen minutes
into lunch and I've got no appetite and don't really
remember hunger pains. Think this is bad and maybe
because of all the intake how was I to know it would
build up a cake and my body knows no other food as I
order and talk myself into consuming for it would be a
waste and on those grounds I should eat. 11:18
am Been back on for a good 18 now the boss of the boss
is lost in a toss with joke strolled broke who happens to
have a spoken touch. He oozes yes he's a
zombie oozer with his webs of words he leaks and tosses
ensnaring all those who would dare to give a naked ear
then he hooks them with symphonic barbs and harpooned
phrasing you have no escape and are cornered. No one
could step in and flip the table on this type of Z-man it's
better to let it pass as the boss realizes and wonders
why did the thought come last. She gives him his cheap
prize and struts to the other end of the room. We begin to
joke and laugh to try and lighten the gloom. The storm
did pass and we can still dance in the rain and for several
moments you feel no pain. 2:44 bamm! There slams the
door. The engine starts and the music sounds, off goes
the hat like the sox's just blew the stadium crowd. In
record time I make the mountains climb think I'm getting
stronger week after week as in front of the class I speak
of my ideas and key philosophies bounce the frequency
so you can see me and not lose me in this moment
because I know somewhere you're out there just like I'm
out here and maybe you're wanting the same of love as

me. Oh got lost in afternoon love songs oldies jams.
"Where have all the flowers" to the one where that man
was talking about his girl. Everyone a different notage all
strike at the strings of your heart with the same pressure
make you wanna open the love that you would forever
long treasure. On too long and I'm on time to class.
I've gotta sit next to the crazy girls today. The guys give
me shit because I don't fit in with the valley vibe I roll
my eyes and give a grin no ties with that tribe. I take my
deep breaths and think of being a kid at home. Then I'm
free and I smile and look down at this invisible A just
like every other day I show up to get my A. I've learned
to see it before it's on me and I admit it reassures me for
even I do get a hint a touch of test fear or anxiety. Again
I'm not blaming the coffee but think, ugh I think I need a
cup of coffee two more answers this has just been a
breeze but now that I'm done I do want some fun I can
squeeze. The nights got time though and I am up for a
quiet walk with myself into the rays of the sun. Dinner
for one the roommate is out tonight and I'm here again in
this light. Oh Stretch was eve 11:10 goodnight.

Chapter 13:Day 13

4:13 a.m. The 13th and tomorrow I get paid. Life seems too good just gotta get through one more day. I sit up in bed and reach to the end of the head. Found myself slept backward so I twist then so I can go forward and still keep my eyes straight so I see where I go tell that crowd thanks but I know. What today is and where I should be took on an extra shift hope I see the greenery and not this dirty apron. Mocha, grinds, vanilla syrup, take my pick hold them up check which one looks less sick because it's too many days straight through and I'm sliding on the socks and out of time with some minute change maybe two. I seat belt pull and straighten up pray to God the fuel is enough for my guy to start up. Twist and close my eyes for the blessing in disguise keys twist and he purrs like my beast take me away and look near my foot and clutch pedal I found a treasure almost like a medal. Money for fuel now I debate which one will help more and not make me late.....should I fuel the tank and check out the food bank. Stomach growls to add it's two cents hope it's not speaking in vain like the a/c trying to vent this overheated car that just doesn't give up. And I look at the time and surprised to my sight it' 13 minutes to my shift with no hints of delight. Pull into the lot and check out all my goods.....my gear, my body, what's on my body, how it feels mmmm don't think too much will have me spinning wheels. I wear my look of courage and smiles hope, hop past the mote full of angry crocodiles, all waiting to start their shift and kiss ass to who they'd sell, but if any opposite sex strolls by, that's when they turn into worldly belles. They should all be due in just after the start of the 12:00 o'clock hour all in search of fame, wealth, and power. Now I'm spinning the drinks on the bar and entertaining the kids and I'm taking requests for songs from the highest bid. They want to hear "fever" because it sounds off from my pipes and enters the air fills their soul and they challenge to think, dream, or dare. Wanting to hear because it leaves them wanting more, connectual interactions all because they came through my door. 10:16 In walks in two sunset wanna be teens what a friend would call forever 21 or at least they want to be, in high pitched annoying tonality like a shrill numbing to the ear, and confound in thought of escape when the chalk and board of black scratch for there is no match. The blenders are threatening a strike and this espresso machine "The beast" has borrowed parts from my bike. I try to stay positive by laws of attraction block out each LA faction that comes to break us, make us take heed to trust for their heart could never bare love only masked lust. Then finally the sweetest of beings comes in to tell the world in this moment we are okay and alright. The man preached out like we were all lost in the night. Only a few dark zombies did peer round the corner trying to hear for all they wanted was drinks and their money to squander. They drink, sip, maybe throw off a trip and waste. Lost and so oblivious they take on a form like previous. Then the man says a few final words the boy at the bar and I wish it was already time for me to fly off to the car. I meet eyes with the man and I am even comforted. He was a saint an angel a guardian of one I could feel no complaint. He came to give me words and peace like a message delivered to me. I knew then in future moments this beings interactions I would share and do speak. He sat to sip his brew an hour passed and he seemed to be through. Then he walked on up to me and handed me a letter. I took it and looked in aww and I think he took pleasure. He turned and walked off to the sunset and I can still remember his name, his eyes, and frame. I gazed around to see who did witness, and I think how can I get a break should I speak of fever or dizziness. I must read this note, I can't just put it away in my tote. "Ah-ha I have it I will go to the bathroom!" It's a single so there will be quiet and no one there to loom. 15 minutes later and then that in tears I have a glow like I've got no cares of fears. This angel wrote me, wrote me a letter in hopes I would smile more and it would evolve me better. I step into the cage and all the worlds a stage and I can feel so much love from the ones here and above and I am in touch in this moment from so many other times and instances for I know my love will come over mountains and far distances. Continue to believe was the messages biggest entail such a beautiful verbal collection I never thought I'd get such mail. 1:00 pm. Off to another session with the homies they play as I sing. In the valley with the heat rolling across with the wind, wide open planes our music rings on, and we cry out like the Indians danced for rain. Love, peace, and of sorrows old and new we hope we keep you free and far from blue. Speak only truth like the bugs would sing about in so many of their songs which I believe in no mix of a library would their songs fit or belong. They stand alone like as we do on this stage like any night this night we play on like each a mage. Let us capture you and hold you in tones of embrace, make you wonder what is this vibe in this place. So calm, so cool, gentle breezes over take the crowd and some of them begin to sing aloud. This cover we all know and by a man with his piano so they sing because it was my song, and their song, and your song…..our song. I drive in at 12:55 Thank God I made it safe sound home and alive. Then I walk in drop the bag tear of my clothes far from jag. Then the water rushes over me and the day begins to wash such golden vivid memories so bright an close to touch. Stand air dry on this warm and sticky night I watch the moon as it watches me alone with the smell of something and candy. I spread out in bed and find a comfortable spot lay my head. Off and into dreams I long like a record that has begun it's song…..hope this gets deep and holds me long. Give me the sweetest dreams because I've got no one, here to say to do I wake you or let you sleep do you need it now more than me oh my gosh my hands just creep because I'm so lost in you….lost in you. Ah but one day you'll be here I believe this to be true. Drift off in dreams as this dream I hope I dream and maybe I see you and meet you there or anywhere as long as we both dream….last clock check at 2:03 ….zzzzzzzzzz. What's every word I know in German, Spanish, or Italian… why are the languages I've learned so distant from where I've come from. Why do the coffees from home seem a little closer to my brewed soul, I know the low acid helps but perhaps there's more in store for those that seek to find. Good food and drink of origins lost in reading as I dust about rainforests I'll never see and jungles my feet may never walk. A drum starts beating on radio in the café, "espresso" is chanted over and over with some rhythmic jungle tones suggesting simple earth and seduction. I roll my eyes just back far enough in the parking spot tonight and my imagination soars through my open window Paine as the rain begins to cross its face I wake from little slips into slumber as I stand in dreamlands line hoping 1 they call my number.

Chapter 14:Day 14

5:11 and I'm very LATE AGAIN!!!! I was supposed to be in at 4:00, why haven't they called why's this water on the floor? The sink not right, now really can't have this, try to wake the roomy so I can be off as I try to shake this cloud it hovers so gloomy and soundtrack side A "death March" like a funeral so eery. I drive, run, walk, to face my doom, What will he say? Ralph's always loaded and ready for the words set on stun. I park in a flash and hop-skip mad-dash and I'm in whew there's no crowd as I know Ralph will blow and bring it loud. I'm so in stun city lock down and I'm pouring my milk I can barely hear but reach for the silk. 5:49 Always a good mix of ingredients I am tossing and this feels bittersweet like I'm a champ once last time in the ring. Then I just let it flow shots around and the room begins to glow. The zombies are on strawberry hill, all bathing in the rich tones of cream and sugar. An eager new barista makes his way out to ensure the environment is friendly and inviting to strangers who would find a moment to share and spend with us in this place. Wow… This is the human race?....So together yet so far apart. Lost in interpretations, self sensations, and translations the signs of our love.They come to be served and cared for given warmth. They come because someone made something for them, and it helps them get by each day. Some of them say, love me then hate me, and others don't lie or mistake me for I am real and see you in this place and I am like no other before you. Then the battlefield sheds it's cold and trudging feel and the stones all around echo chants and there is light and love on the battlefield. We have brought it here with smiles and cheer and this notion has me lost, lost in this moment. Smile sky high in this moment so sublime on the ride rolling by and everything's alright. Ralph could be frantic with screams while I'm off lost in clouds and dreams. It rushes over me and feels so right this morning feels so right like we're on a set cruise on a voyage lost in the ocean and we make the best of it and feel free like we're on some adventuresome filled spree. Deep breaths channel me back to reality for the scene has gotten me pulled. Like an extra on a set I Don't wanna be, forced to push up the bra, show big teeth, and impose sexy. Sexy because I want to be, on my ground and terms, gated of sure-it's-me like seas flow so freely. Won't care if he doesn't see, for all that matters is I see me. I have collected and gathered all the dimensions and data of the stone diamond that I am so that I may show this world and shape it through my edges as inevitable as commercials of sipping on corona's with wedges. 9:00 a.m. I'm sent off on a break for my wheels have been over spun, fingers burned, so they tell me to grab a drink and run quick to the back of the store behind the swinging small window door. I sit and it's silent aside for the washer that is cleaning the metal ware from the last 4 hours. All seems to have been going well this morning even without the commotion I was showing to self on the drive, swallowed down my heart so I could stay alive. I gaze around the room at the notes and signs then fixate on the schedule seek out names find mine, I've been changed for today and realize I'm not late. Then a moment of blissful joy I see him walk in, the mail man and he's got checks. I smile back and take a deep inhale look back on the last two weeks like a book a tale I should regale. I slice open the envelope like it held the meaning of hope and I look down at the digits and smile for this is what I've come to all the while. Now I'm untying my apron strings and feeling thoughts of lost folly, and I remember a day when worries to come were of only to play with which dolly. I have lived through my days here and are ready to sail on out the door stand next to the curb as a cab I hale…..but oh wait stop this mellow melon collie shot in a movie I drove here, and am ready to go, and can leave when I want to leave. I take out a pen and piece of paper begin to dash on the lines as my thoughts start to spiral to somewhere down deeper. Then it all poured out like a bold Columbian roast and I reached for my cup and the computer screen I did toast. I raised up the page and looked down at my wage and smiled again, oh how I'll never have to come back here again. I took off my hat and let my hair down the scent of jasmine and Kona coffee went so decadent to me oh how I'd pair it with slice of cake perhaps strawberry….with maybe some cream frosting for it can't be resisted, then thoughts of cream have me grinning with lips of so twisted. Then I strut out of the back like a fox ready to attack but smiling with coy delight as I know this day Ralph or the boy named Sue won't put up a fight, Then the last stroll out and a peace brews within and I'm lost in delight. Birds are singing off high in the trees, the sun is shining and I'm coming down the hill and I can see all of LA one wishes for such views and such a clear day and then set scan as I laugh and smile no way no tears from a crocodile. On the band a disco song plays for all of two measures, then a slow deep song, to a rocking treasure, I tap to the beat of the song and I smile like I know all along right or wrong we all belong and shall go on……and the clock tick tocks on and on.

Epilogue

This book symbolizes a a moment that I took to write down the feelings and cryptic moments that came from a venture into a a world of coffee in L.A. I never wanted to think bad on my time or remember the worst of the times. Their logo is everywhere and I never wanted that signal of harsh moments or questions. So this book is an embodiment of energy, people, and stories. This was my way to say goodbye and to reach my end with coffee and being it's bar wench. This company gave me both opportunity and experience like no other. I can say the healing method for this book has worked ever since the day I wrote it. I am still able to drink every now and then with the company and never have too many hard feelings from my days as a partner, leader, and in many meetings mentioned as, "Zen". So many worthy people. I can say I remember so many faces and names and times. Even a few friends worked with me for the company and we spent cherished memories together getting defeated in the trenches. So many of us have gone off into the wind and allowed it to take us to places we would never dream.

With the time, we have taken the excellence we cultivated in those times and used it to achieve, build, and create a walk closer to our dreams and goals. I'm so very proud of so many of you that I got to meet whether a day a few hours, a few moments, some of your souls still highlight such an amazing time of people and coffee. A time that was right before the housing market crash and just after 9/11. So many great people and shining faces.

Thank you for letting me be your leading lady in the story and reminding me that even though our paths may never cross the memory and the words are always so very important. Here's to your lives and your loves may they be surrounded with light and joy.

My hopes are that you buy a book for someone after reading this and have a couple conversations about reading and visit your favorite book over a cup of coffee. Join and share with me online via Memoirs of a Barista on social media.

Coffee Notes Space for you <3